THE GHOSTLY PARADOX

PARANORMAL ADVENTURES FOR YOUNG MINDS

M.A. PELKEY

Book Cover by Matthew Pelkey

Illustrations by Melise Bricault

First edition 2023

CONTENTS

CHAPTER 1

The Intriguing Invitation

It was a typical day in the charming little town of Pickleton. Matt, a twelve-year-old boy who adores adventure and spending time with his best friend Kaylee, was playing a game of fetch with his faithful canine companion, Dash. As Dash eagerly pursued a thrown stick, he stumbled upon something strange poking out from their mailbox.

Among the plain envelopes that contained Mom and Dad's mail, there was a unique and eye-catching letter sticking out. The letter was sealed with wax, as kings used to do in ancient times. It was positioned at the perfect height for Dash to reach up and grab. Dash eagerly ran over to Matt with the mysterious envelope in his mouth, dropping it at his feet. Looking up at Matt, Dash wagged his tail, hoping to receive a treat for his hard work.

Matt looked down and noticed that the letter had his name on it! With anticipation, he swiftly tore the envelope open and began reading aloud, "You are cordially invited to join us at 4357 Fallacy Circle for fun and ADVENTURE!" Hearing those words, Matt's eyes widened with excitement. He knew exactly where 4357 Fallacy Circle was. In fact, the entire town was aware of its location—the abandoned haunted mansion on the outskirts of town. Well, supposedly haunted, at least. If the mention of "ADVENTURE" wasn't enticing enough, the opportunity to explore the old mansion certainly was. Overwhelmed by curiosity, he dashed next door to share the thrilling news with his best friend, Kaylee. As Kaylee laid her eyes on the invitation, her excitement became visible, matching Matt's catchy enthusiasm and giddiness.

Filled with enthusiasm, Matt and Kaylee wholeheartedly agreed to explore the mansion. Dash, showing his agreement, wagged his tail vigorously and let out a series of excited barks. Little did they know that this thrilling adventure would not only test their reasoning skills but also change the life of a complete stranger for the better!

CHAPTER 2

The Ghost of 4357 Fallacy Circle

As the sun rose in the eastern sky, Matt, Kaylee, and Dash nervously looked up at the creepy abandoned mansion. The old building hadn't felt a human's touch for many years. Vines grew on its rotting walls, shingles lay scattered on the roof, and boards blocked every window. The only sounds that reached the trio were the eerie hoot of a barn owl in the distance and the occasional whisper of the wind through the trees. The familiar rush of adrenaline pulsed through their veins as they cautiously approached the sinister, decaying structure.

They opened the door to the main entryway and were completely awestruck by the beautiful craftsmanship showcased throughout the house. Despite its run-down exterior, the interior was a breathtaking sight. However, their fascination was short-lived. While their eyes followed the grand staircase rising on both sides of the entryway, they caught sight of an eerie, ghostly figure blanketed in mist, which appeared out of context.

It was a ghost! Dash was so frightened that he hid behind Matt's legs, shaking uncontrollably. Kaylee appeared interested by the apparition, while Matt simply stared in disbelief. The ghost started speaking, its voice echoing through the cobweb-filled, elaborate entryway. It communicated through riddles that inexplicably repeated themselves. Matt whispered to Kaylee, "It seems trapped in a continuous loop!" The ghost flew back and forth uttering the same words. Each time it finished, a sigh escaped the ghost, and the cycle would begin again.

Confused, Matt, Kaylee, and Dash stood mesmerized as the ghost repeated its mysterious routine. They sensed a profound connection between the repeated phrase and the ghost's motions, but what could it mean? Always prepared, Kaylee reached into her pocket, pulled out her notebook, and hastily copied the phrase: "I haunt this hall because I am a ghost. I am a ghost because I haunt this hallway." With a shared determination to uncover the truth, they agreed to delve deeper into the mansion. Well, Kaylee and Matt were eager to explore, but Dash shook in fear, desperately tugging at the back of Matt's pants in an attempt to persuade the foolish human from venturing closer to danger. Possessing an uncanny sixth sense for mysteries, Kaylee and Matt remained undeterred.

Something bizarre was unfolding with the ghost, and they were determined in their quest to free it from whatever wicked force held it captive.

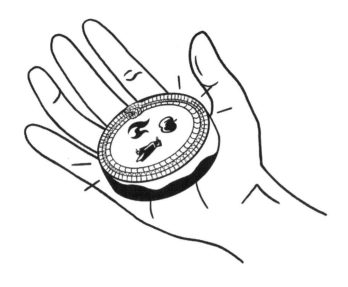

CHAPTER 3

The Circular Artifact

Matt, Kaylee, and Dash observed as the ghost veered off its usual path, prompting them to follow its repetitive movements down the hall. As they proceeded, they couldn't help but notice the rooms they passed appeared frozen in time, their beauty preserved despite the layers of dust and cobwebs. However, as they approached the room at the end of the hallway, their attention was grabbed by an odd object that stood out within the stillness. It was a spherical clay disk reminiscent of an artifact discovered at an archaeological dig site. Complex markings were carved in its center, while a snake-like creature coiled around the entire circumference, its head devouring its own tail. Strangely, the artifact remained untouched by dust or spider webs, almost as if it possessed a life of its own. Casting an eerie, pale light, the circular self-consuming snake seemed to fill the room with a ghostly light.

As they drew closer to the spherical disk, the ghost's voice grew more distinct, echoing in their ears. The ghost's strange movements echoed the patterns of its recurring riddles and repetitive motions. It became increasingly apparent that the ghost's very existence and purpose were intricately tied to this puzzling artifact. But what could be the nature of this connection?

They observed something peculiar as they studied the artifact more closely. It seemed to distort the surrounding light and environment. Moreover, the closer they approached it, the stronger the sensation of déjà vu intensified. The spherical disk, much like the ghost's words and actions, appeared trapped in a loop. This instilled Dash with an unsettling feeling. He refused to give up on pulling them back to safety. Dash moved away from Matt's pants and began tugging at Kaylee's pants instead. In response, Kaylee leaned forward, planted a gentle kiss behind Dash's ear, and asked, "Are you trying to protect us, you brave little boy?" Encouraged by her tenderness, Dash slowly let go of the garment and stood between the two investigators with his senses on high alert.

Overwhelmed and bewildered by the day's events, Matt and Kaylee recognized the importance of seeking assistance in unraveling the puzzle. They wanted answers. With that in mind, they departed and made their way home with the intension of visiting the library tomorrow, the sole central repository of knowledge in Pickleton.

CHAPTER 4

Unraveling the Mystery

The following day, Matt and Kaylee visited the town library to meet with Mrs. Kimberlee, the respected librarian well-known for her knowledge, wisdom, and kindness. They believed that she held the key to understanding their dilemma. Accompanying them, as always, was Dash, their fearless protector, companion, and fellow paranormal detective.

Mrs. Kimberlee's hazel eyes brimmed with genuine interest as she patiently listened to the tale shared by the trio. Even Dash had a thing or two to contribute, expressing his thoughts through grumbles and barks. Taking a deep breath, Mrs. Kimberlee contemplated the story and concluded that the ghost appeared to be trapped in a cycle of circular reasoning.

"Circular reasoning," she said, "is a logical error." Mrs. Kimberlee continued to provide further clarification, "When someone commits this logical fallacy, they basically start with the conclusion they are attempting to prove." Glancing around the library, she offered a simple illustration, saying, "Here's an example: Books are essential for learning to read. The only way to learn to read is through books!" She then glanced down at Dash and added, "It's similar to a dog endlessly chasing its own tail, going around in circles without making any progress." Matt and Kaylee's eyes widened in astonishment as they exchanged glances. "Or," the kids screamed, "It's like a snake attempting to eat its own tail!" Overwhelmed with a renewed sense of achievement, the two children dashed off, and Dash joyfully bounded after them.

Matt and Kaylee possessed a deep understanding of the enigma surrounding the mansion. They understood that the ghost, the cryptic phrase, and the circular artifact were all a representation of circular reasoning. It appeared that flawed reasoning was the very force holding the ghost in captivity. Filled with determination, Kaylee passionately declared that they must take action to assist and free the ghost, breaking the cycle once and for all. However, Matt wore a puzzled expression, his brows furrowing in thought. He couldn't grasp the connection between the circular artifact and the ghost. Why did it seem that the two were connected?

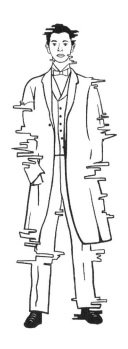

CHAPTER 5

Stopping the First Loop

Matt, Kaylee, and Dash made their way back to 4357 Fallacy Circle, equipped with the knowledge taught by Mrs. Kimberlee and a renewed determination. The mansion seemed less sinister and more like a mystifying puzzle—one reminiscent of the puzzles found in the school library. Kaylee had a particular love for puzzle books and excelled at unraveling logic-based problems.

Dash trotted with a lively bounce in his step, wagging his tail with unrelenting enthusiasm upon catching the scent of the old mansion. His human companions shared a similar feeling. During their initial visit to the mansion, they were gripped by an undeniable sense of fear, similar to the anticipation felt before boarding on a roller-coaster ride. However, this time around, the fear had dissipated. In fact, they now felt some sympathy for the ghost, seeing him as harmless. But was this a misjudgment? Should they still maintain a prudent level of fear? Matt considered these thoughts as they advanced along the path leading to the mansion.

They swung open the grand front door of the mansion, and Dash dashed inside, running up the stairs and racing down the hallway with unwavering determination. Matt and Kaylee rushed to catch up with their four-legged friend. Finally, Dash came to a stop before the circular artifact, assuming an alert stance, his posture perfect, and his ears perked up, attentively pointing forward. It was as if Dash possessed an innate understanding that the trio stood on the edge of a significant discovery.

The ghost circled in front of the circular artifact, repeating its mysterious phrase. Dash tilted his head curiously, spellbound by the riddles. The adorable pup's presence lifted the atmosphere, prompting laughter from the children as they delighted in his adorable antics.

Inspired by Dash's calm demeanor, Kaylee took a step forward, breaking the first loop by pointing out the flaw in the ghost's phrase. "You are not a ghost because you haunt this hallway!" Kaylee shouted. "And you do not haunt this hallway because you are a ghost! That argument is circular and self-defeating. You are a ghost because you passed on from this life and got trapped by your faulty logic. Just because you are a ghost doesn't mean you have to haunt!" Kaylee explained with unwavering confidence. Just then, the ghost stopped, gradually losing its transparency. They weren't able to see through the ghost anymore. It became more translucent, revealing the shades and colors of light behind it but no details. Although no longer transparent, the ghost retained a certain ghostly quality. Dash growled in satisfaction, his bark echoing throughout the grand hall.

Dash drew Matt and Kaylee's attention by barking at the artifact. They noticed that the light originating from the circular artifact had grown dimmer and was pulsating at a slower rate. This revelation sparked a new realization. There was a significant connection between the artifact and the ghost's cycles, but the reason behind it remained unknown. "Dash seems to have a keen instinct for solving these mysteries," Matt remarked.

Their victory filled them with a rush of excitement. Dash pranced around, delighted by his contribution to the team's efforts. The victory boosted their confidence, inflated their egos, and left their spirits soaring. However, despite their delight, the trio was aware that this mystery was far from resolved. The ghost still lingered, and in a surprising turn of events, it seemed to be glitching!

CHAPTER 6

The Artifact Multiplies

Matt, Kaylee, and Dash gazed at the ghost in curiosity. Suddenly, it multiplied from one into three distinct apparitions. Dash barked forcefully at the artifact, which also copied itself. Now, there were three ghosts and three circular artifacts! Each ghost bore a striking resemblance to the other, but they spoke different words. Ghost one repeated, "I am just a child! I can't be freed until I grow up!" The second ghost declared, "I am a man! I must provide for my family!" The third ghost mumbled, "I have learned so much! I want to teach my grandkids my life's lessons!" Matt looked at Kaylee, a hint of worry in his eyes. "Oh no! We've made it worse! He has split into three different ghosts!" Kaylee stood there, her face reflecting a puzzled expression. Matt continued, "This isn't circular reasoning; it's regret! It seems like he regrets the choices he made throughout his life. But... all three ghosts look exactly the same...kind of...Just at different ages!"

Just then, the two kids noticed that Dash wasn't next to them! In a panic, they looked around and saw him at the far end of the room, next to the bed. "Dash, are you tired, bud?" Matt said, with a hint of amusement in his voice. "No!" Kaylee screamed. "Look, he's looking at that picture!" She was right. Next to the bed sat a small old-fashion picture. They recognized the person in the picture too. It resembled the three ghosts flying around the room. Matt rushed over to the picture and picked it up. As he stared closely at the front, Kaylee noticed something on the back. It was a date. It read, "Revolvius Loopmire - April 7, 1898."

Kaylee gazed at the date, then at the three ghosts, and finally at the picture. "I've got it!" she yelled, excitement filling her voice. Startled, Matt and Dash both screamed, "Ahhhh!"

CHAPTER 7

Breaking the Curse

Matt hurriedly caught up to Kaylee, sprinting towards the trio of apparitions, with Dash not far behind him. "What do you mean?" Matt exclaimed, trying to keep up with her thoughts. Kaylee turned to Matt, a big smile on her face, and said, "Remember what Mrs. Kimberlee said about this logical error?" Matt nodded, a awkward smile indicating he remembered but wasn't quite sure where she was going with this. Curiosity heightened; he urged her to explain. "She said it's a logical fallacy that circles in on itself," Kaylee explained, her excitement evident in her voice. "Correct!" she exclaimed triumphantly. Matt looked puzzled and voiced his doubts, "He's just expressing his desire to complete certain aspects of his life. I don't see anything circular about it." Kaylee's grin grew sly as she replied, "It's a logical error where the argument loops back on itself! Mrs. Kimberlee never said the argument had to be fully verbalized!"

All of a sudden, Matt's eyes brightened up, a spark of realization in them. Dash, seemingly understanding the excitement, positioned himself next to Matt with his chest puffed out and his skinny tail wagging back and forth. Matt glanced down at Dash and gave him a quick pet, then turned his attention to Kaylee, offering her a compliment. "Nice thinking! Mrs. Kimberlee would be proud!" he said. Taking a deep breath, Matt looked up at the three ghosts, his voice slightly trembling, "Um... Excuse me, sirs... I mean, Mr. Loopmire!" In that moment, the three ghosts stopped their eerie movements and turned to face them, wearing expressions of melancholy.

Kaylee spoke up with confidence, addressing the young Mr. Loopmire, "Your thinking is flawed, sir. You believe that you are still a child and will only be freed once you grow up. But in reality, you have already lived a full life!" Matt chimed in, supporting Kaylee's point, "Exactly! According to that logic, you should already be freed!" At that moment, the ghost in question paused and appeared puzzled, its confusion evident in its ghostly features.

They regarded the second ghost with newfound confidence. Matt was the first to speak, "You no longer need to provide for your family. In fact, you have already done everything you can for them." The ghost's expression softened in response. Kaylee then spoke, her voice filled with compassion, "Based on your own reasoning, you should already be liberated. You were once a man a century ago, and now you are a spirit who needs to move on."

Finally, they turned their gaze to the third ghost, their expressions filled with care and concern. Speaking in a gentle and compassionate tone, they explained to him that his predicament stemmed from his professed duty to share his wisdom. The ghost appeared to acknowledge the truth in their words but grew motionless upon hearing that his wisdom had already been passed down through generations. Kaylee spoke, "Based on your own reasoning, you should already find peace, as your wisdom has been successfully shared."

Just then, a bright flash illuminated the room. Matt and Kaylee instinctively covered their eyes, shielding themselves from the blinding scene, while Dash sought refuge behind Matt. When they cautiously glanced back at the spot where the three apparitions had stood, they found that only one remained. Their attention then shifted to the three circular artifacts, only to discover that they had vanished. Mr. Loopmire's form was no longer ethereal or translucent; he now stood before them in a solid, opaque state. As he turned his gaze towards Matt, Kaylee, and Dash, he expressed his appreciation. Suddenly, a radiant light beamed through the roof, casting its glow upon Mr. Loopmire. Looking up at the light, a smile graced his face—an unfamiliar sight to the trio. Amidst their amazement, they heard a warm chuckle arise from him, and then he vanished into the warm glow of the light, leaving only echoes of his presence behind.

CHAPTER 8

The Day After Christmas

The mood of the old mansion changed immediately after the ghost was freed. The rooms appeared brighter, and the air felt lighter and easier to breathe. The mansion almost seemed to exhale with joy as a gust of wind swept through its halls. On their way out, Dash halted, turned around, and trotted back towards the stairs. He lifted his leg as if to say, "I came, I saw, I conquered!" Matt and Kaylee chuckled at the proud little puppy.

As they walked down the path from the house, Kaylee turned towards Matt and began to explain, "The ghost was trapped in an endless cycle of faulty thinking, unable to break free from it." Matt nodded in agreement and replied, "Absolutely! Let's make sure we don't fall into the same pattern of faulty thinking!"

Despite Dash's lack of understanding regarding the conversation between Kaylee and Matt, he wagged his tail enthusiastically, as if he were an active participant in their conversation. His joyful response added a charming touch to the moment, further highlighting his inclusion as a cherished member of their group.

"With pride," Kaylee declared, "we were able to assist him in breaking free from that cycle. We demonstrated to him the flaws in his logic. We've witnessed how poor reasoning can ensnare someone in a never-ending loop, and I'm determined to prevent that from happening to us or anyone we care about!"

As the kids continued to discuss the events of the day, Dash's attention was quickly diverted by a passing squirrel. His enthusiastic barking interrupted the moment, causing both Kaylee and Matt to burst into laughter. They watched with amusement as Dash spun in circles, attempting to catch his own tail. Seizing the opportunity created by Dash's playful antics, the clever squirrel took advantage of the distraction and swiftly scampered up a nearby tree.

Their adventure had come to an end, and they always felt a slight sense of letdown after such grand missions, similar to the day after Christmas. The anticipation built up throughout the year, only to be swiftly over. However, much like Christmas, they were aware that another adventure awaited just around the corner.

CHAPTER 9

The Next Invitation

After their encounter at the mansion, Matt, Kaylee, and Dash all agreed to keep their peculiar ghostly adventure a secret. After all, who in the world would believe that they had successfully freed a ghost from an eternal cycle of flawed reasoning?

About a month later, while immersed in a video game session in Kaylee's living room, Dash's ears perked up at something catching his attention. He darted towards the window, emitting a joyful bark, and then turned his head as if to signal, "Look, guys!" Intrigued, Matt lifted his head to see what had captured

Dash's excitement. It turned out to be the mailman, an ordinary sight that initially seemed unremarkable. Matt was about to resume his seat when his gaze fell upon a small, distinctive envelope, instantly grabbing his attention. A mix of excitement and anxiety compelled Matt to let out a yelp. Startled, Kaylee turned to see what had stirred such a reaction and quickly noticed the same extraordinary envelope. Their eyes met, including Dash's, and without hesitation, they bolted out of the house, racing towards the mailbox in a rush of anticipation.

Dash, being a whippet which was the fastest breed of his size, reached the mailbox first, snatched the letter, and dashed back inside, leaving the clumsy humans to stumble over each other in their chase. Once they regrouped in the living room, Dash dropped the letter onto the floor and glanced up with anticipation, eagerly awaiting a treat. Kaylee picked up the letter and began to read, her eyes lighting up as she recognized the distinctive style of the writing. Matt's attention was drawn to the letter's return address, which he whispered in a hushed tone, "Dreadwood." Kaylee's eyes widened as she exclaimed, "They're facing an outbreak of... zombies!" Matt shifted his gaze downwards and noticed familiar markings on the letter—a strange watermark consisting of mysterious symbols, identical to those found at the center of the circular artifact they had encountered. The question loomed before them: What could these symbols possibly signify?

Dash's tail wagged with uncontrolled excitement at the prospect of yet another adventure. Suddenly, a small voice emerged from behind them, exclaiming, "Did someone mention zombies?" Matt and Kaylee swiftly turned around to find Makenna, Kaylee's younger sister, standing there with hopeful eyes. Makenna's face lit up as they confirmed that she could join them on this upcoming journey. Makenna possessed an adventurous spirit that rivaled the combined daring of both Matt and Kaylee, making her an ideal companion for their thrilling journeys.

Just then, they heard a small screech and faint scratches, followed by a sudden bark. They turned their gaze towards the backyard, where Kaylee couldn't help but chuckle at the sight of Dash in hot pursuit of a squirrel, leaping up a tree. "I guess we can rely on Dash! He's already sharpening his zombie-chasing abilities," Kaylee remarked with a playful tone. The trio laughed and ended the day by planning how they were going to embark on this next adventure.

To Be Continued

Stay Sharp with Kaylee and Matt

Practice your ability to recognize circular reasoning, just like Matt and Kaylee! Keep your mind sharp, and you'll be able to spot the circular reasoning fallacy too!

Example 1:

Person 1: "Why do you believe that Matt is trustworthy?"

Person 2: "He always tells the truth."

Person 1: "How do you know that?"

Person 2: "Because he is trustworthy."

In this example, Matt's trustworthiness is being used as evidence for why he always tells the truth. However, there is no external evidence provided to support the initial claim of Matt's trustworthiness. The argument becomes circular as it relies on itself without any additional justification.

Example 2: This book is popular because everyone likes it.

This statement demonstrates circular reasoning by using the book's popularity as the reason for why it is well-liked. However, this explanation lacks external evidence or an independent source to validate the book's popularity. To avoid circular reasoning, it is necessary to provide additional support or objective factors that contribute to the book's widespread appeal.

Example 3: "My teacher is smart because she knows a lot."

This statement commits a circular argument by using the teacher's knowledge to justify her intelligence, and vice versa. The reasoning relies on a circular loop, where intelligence is equated to knowing a lot, which is then used to justify intelligence. To avoid circular reasoning, it would be essential to provide objective criteria or external evidence that demonstrates the teacher's intelligence beyond her knowledge alone.

Kaylee

Introduction:

Name: Kaylee Sinclair

Age: 12

Birthday: November 1, 2010

Personality Traits:

Logical and analytical: Kaylee developed her sharp logic skills as a little girl. When she was eight years old, she had an intense love for Harry Potter and wanted her parents to take her to a summer replay of the first three movies at the local theater. Not wanting to go, her parents presented her with a puzzle and told her that if she solved it, they would take her. She effortlessly solved the problem, and as a result, her parents kept their end of the deal. Here is the logic problem that she solved. Can you solve it?

Matt, Kaylee, and Makenna went camping, and each brought a different item. The items were a book, a bottle of water, and a plunger. Let's use the clues to determine who brought what:

1. *Makenna didn't bring the plunger.*

2. *Kaylee didn't bring the book.*

3. *Matt brought the water.*

Caring and Empathetic: One day after recess at the age of ten, all the kids came back into the classroom and began picking on a girl named Jill. Her hair was all messy, her legs were covered in dirt, and she smelled like she had been sweating. Jill had been playing gaga ball with a bunch of boys on the playground. Kaylee looked at Jill and thought that she looked and smelled just like the boys. This made her chuckle and join in laughing at Jill.

Later that night, Kaylee was in dance class with her friends when she started to practice her triple spin. On her third spin, she pushed so hard to get her leg up high that she accidentally let out a loud fart! The entire class burst into laughter. Then, they started choking as the gas cloud reached their noses. Kaylee felt terribly embarrassed.

Later that night, she thought to herself, "Why did they laugh at me? Everyone farts! If everyone farts, why did they insist on making me feel bad when I farted?" Then it hit her. She had done the same thing to Jill earlier that day. Just like Kaylee, Jill had fallen victim to the cruel nature of young humans. Jill was sweaty, just like all other humans get after exercise. However, for some reason, all the other kids, who also get stinky from time to time, began picking on her and made her feel very alone.

It was at that point that Kaylee decided to apologize to Jill and to never be mean to people again. After all, we are all human, and we all crave love and respect.

Kaylee's Favorites:

1. Favorite color

Purple

2. Favorite number

27 – She doesn't know why; she just likes the number. She says that it just looks right!

3. Best Friend

Matt Elkin

4. Favorite food

Watermelon

5. Favorite day of the week

Saturday! Because that is when all the real adventure for the week takes place!

6. What does Kaylee want to be when she grows up?

A paranormal scientist!

7. If she had one superpower what would it be? Telekinesis! She says life would be easier if she could just think and a plate of watermelon would come floating towards her.

MATT

Introduction:

Name: Matt Elkin

Age: 12

Birthday: November 11, 2010

Personality Traits:

Intelligent and curious: Matt has been curious ever since he can remember. When he was a boy, he enjoyed watching his parents change the brakes on the car, clean the carburetor on the lawn mower, and even build a shed in their backyard. By the time Matt turned nine-years-old, he already had a large collection of books and tools. He loves knowing how things work. One time, during fourth grade, he overheard his teacher talking about how slow her laptop was. Politely, he asked if he could take a look at it. Within ten minutes, Matt had the computer running at top speed. The teacher was so thankful that she allowed him to pick a reward from the classroom treasure chest. Later that year, Matt learned how to write and read in binary for fun. Here is the first code that he wrote to Kaylee in binary.

01000011 01100001 01110010 01110000 01100101
00100000 01000100 01101001 01100101 01101101

Can you break the code? You may need to search for the meaning of the word once you discover what the word is!

Adventurous and courageous: Matt is full of adventure and courage, except when he is around snakes, spiders, and things that ooze. He tells Kaylee that he got his courage from the cat he used to have as a younger boy. She laughed at first, thinking he was joking. However, he emphatically told her that it used to be his job to change the litter in the litter box, which exposed him to toxoplasma gondii. Kaylee thought he had just made it up until she Googled the term. As it turns out, it is a parasite found in cat waste and can cause risk-taking behavior! Strange!

Matt's Favorites:

1. Favorite color

Blue

2. Favorite number

3 – He says it just feels right! You can tell that he and Kaylee are friends! They have the same answer for their numbers!

3. Best Friend

Kaylee Sinclair

4. Favorite food

Apple Pie

5. Favorite day of the week

Saturday – That is the day you work your week through
school to get to!

6. What does Matt want to be when he grows up?

No clue!

7. If he had one superpower what would it be?

The ability to fly! How cool would that be?

MAKENNA

Introduction:

Name: Makenna Sinclair

Age: 7

Birthday: April 1, 2016

Personality Traits:

Fearless and intelligent: Makenna's bravery and fearlessness stem from watching her older sister and Matt embark on daring adventures. She yearns to be part of the group so badly that she willingly dives into danger to prove herself. Last year, Matt, Kaylee, and Makenna were happily jumping on the trampoline, playing trampoline basketball. Matt and Kaylee became concerned that they were jumping too high for Makenna, fearing she might get hurt. But Makenna was determined not to let them stop on her account. She seized the basketball, jumped as hard as she could, and with all her strength, aimed for the hoop to make the shot. To Matt and Kaylee's astonishment, Makenna missed the hoop entirely with the ball but, unexpectedly, managed to make the basket with her own body! There she was, suspended in mid-air, with her rear end sticking through the hoop. Her little feet kicked playfully, trying to free herself, while her voice squeaked with laughter!

Famous for her one-liners: Makenna has been delivering witty remarks since the age of three, leaving even the crustiest of old men in stitches. No one in her family possesses this type of humor, making her ability all the more intriguing. In the upcoming book, you'll get to experience firsthand some of her hilarious one-liners! Speaking of which, do you have any favorite one-liners to share?

Makenna's Favorites:

1. Favorite color

Blue

2. Favorite number

7 – Because that is her age!

3. Best Friend

Dash

4. Favorite food

Pizza

5. Favorite day of the week

Friday

6. What does Makenna want to be when she grows up?

Police officer

7. If she had one superpower what would it be?

Fly

DASH

Introduction:

Name: Dash

Age: 2

Birthday: October 16, 2020

Personality Traits:

Breed: Dash is a Whippet, a sighthound closely related to the greyhound. Whippets hold the title of the fastest breed in their size category, reaching impressive speeds of up to 35 miles per hour. These dogs boast intelligence, a calm demeanor, and a strong affection for snuggling. Due to their lean physique with minimal fat, they expend energy quickly, often leading to relaxed lounging for the remainder of the day. Whippets make excellent family dogs and are generally low-maintenance in terms of care.

Dash, the lovable pooch, serves as the book's primary source of comic relief. He thoroughly enjoys spending time with his beloved human family, showcasing his unique and comical personality. On occasion, Dash amuses the group by conversing in his very own dog language. Although his barks and noises may seem mysterious, Kaylee has managed to decipher some of his signals and is determined to persuade Matt into creating a doggy translator. Care to uncover the secrets behind Dash's messages? Let's give it a try!

1. Rrr, Rrr, Bark, Bark

2. Rrr, Rrr, Rrr

3. Rrr, Rrr

4. Bark, Bark, Bark, Bark, Bark

5. Bark, Bark

6. Bark

7. Bark, Bark, Bark

Dog Morse Code Key (Dog Sounds):

A - Bark, Rrr

B - Bark, Bark, Bark, Bark, Bark

C - Bark, Bark, Bark, Bark, Rrr, Bark, Rrr

D - Bark, Bark, Bark, Bark, Rrr

E - Bark

F - Bark, Bark, Bark, Bark, Bark, Rrr, Bark

G - Rrr, Rrr, Bark

H - Bark, Bark, Bark, Bark, Bark, Bark

I - Bark, Bark

J - Bark, Rrr, Rrr, Rrr

K - Rrr, Bark, Rrr

L - Bark, Rrr, Bark, Bark

M - Rrr, Rrr

N - Rrr, Bark

O - Rrr, Rrr, Rrr

P - Bark, Rrr, Rrr, Bark

Q - Rrr, Rrr, Bark, Rrr

R - Bark, Rrr, Bark

S - Bark, Bark, Bark

T - Rrr

U - Bark, Bark, Rrr

V - Bark, Bark, Bark, Rrr

W - Bark, Rrr, Rrr

X - Rrr, Bark, Bark, Rrr

Y - Rrr, Bark, Rrr, Rrr

Z - Rrr, Rrr, Bark, Bark

Made in United States
Troutdale, OR
11/26/2023